I0815497

★★★★★

MLB TEAMS

# Arizona DIAMONDBACKS

KENNY ABDO

Fly!
An Imprint of Abdo Zoom
abdobooks.com

**abdobooks.com**

Published by Abdo Zoom, a division of ABDO, P.O. Box 398166, Minneapolis, Minnesota 55439. 

Printed in the United States of America, North Mankato, Minnesota.
102025
012026

Photo Credits: AP Images, Bridgeman Images, Getty Images, Shutterstock
Production Contributors: Kenny Abdo, Jennie Forsberg, Grace Hansen
Design Contributors: Candice Keimig, Neil Klinepier

**Library of Congress Control Number: 2025936783**

**Publisher's Cataloging-in-Publication Data**

Names: Abdo, Kenny, author.
Title: Arizona Diamondbacks / by Kenny Abdo
Description: Minneapolis, Minnesota : Abdo Zoom, 2026 | Series: MLB teams | Includes online resources and index.
Identifiers: ISBN 9798384940081 (lib. bdg.) | ISBN 9798384940845 (ebook) | ISBN 9798384941224 (read-to-me ebook)
Subjects: LCSH: Arizona Diamondbacks (Baseball team)--Juvenile literature. | Baseball teams--Juvenile literature. | Professional sports--Juvenile literature. | Sports franchises--Juvenile literature. | Major League Baseball (Organization)--Juvenile literature.
Classification: DDC 796.357--dc23

# Table of CONTENTS

# DIAMONDBACKS

The Arizona sun shines bright on the Diamondbacks' exciting history and famous players.

The team, known to its fans as the D-backs and *Los Serpientes* (Spanish for "snakes"), has supplied legendary pitchers and a World Series win.

CARROLL
7
FIELD
DIAMONDBACKS
fry's
CARRO
CARRO

# BATTER UP!

The Diamondbacks were founded in 1998, making them one of the newest teams in Major League Baseball (MLB). Though the team is **relatively** new, they have a lot to be proud of.

ARIZONA
18

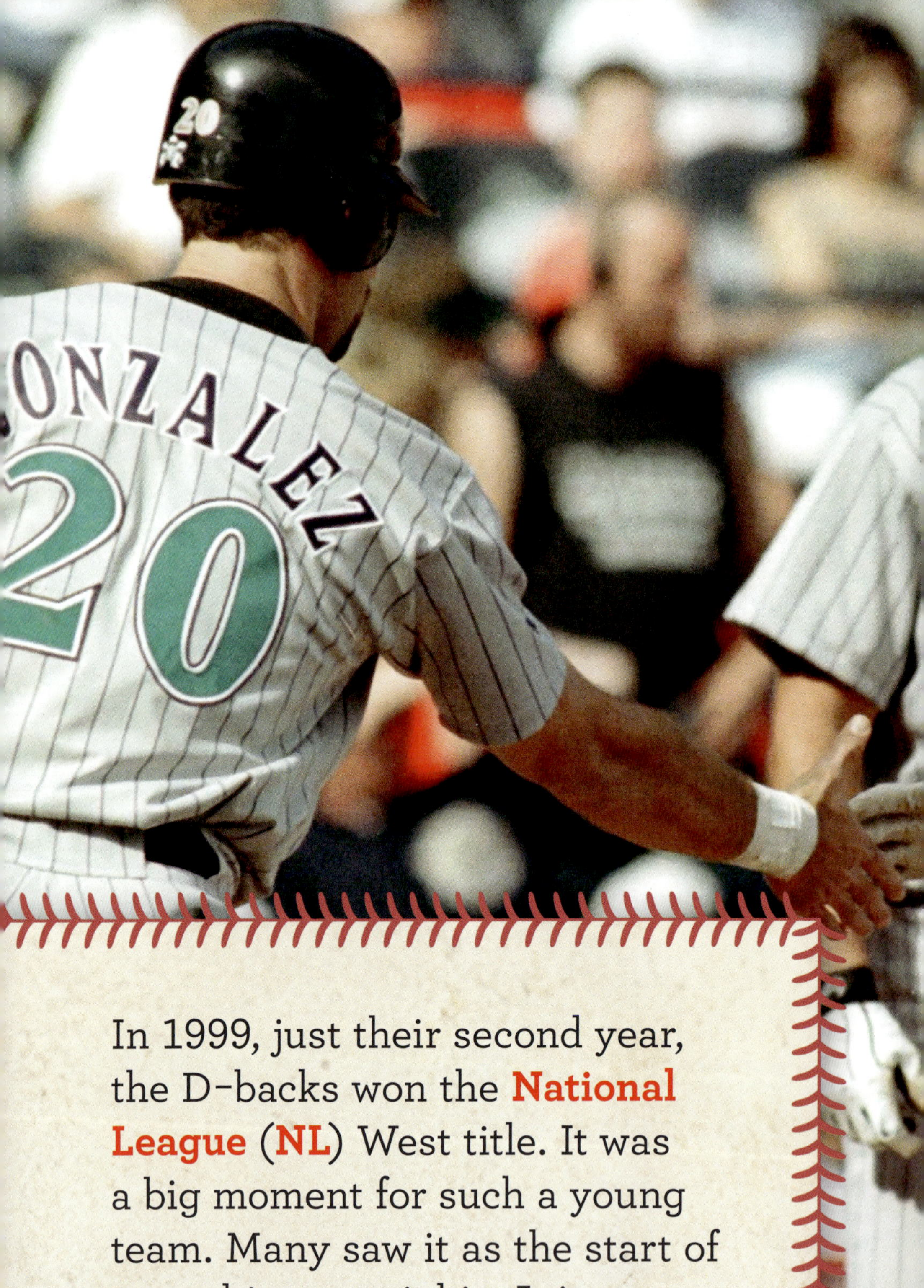


In 1999, just their second year, the D-backs won the **National League** (**NL**) West title. It was a big moment for such a young team. Many saw it as the start of something special in Arizona.

ARIZONA
9
EASTON

The D-backs kept improving in their third season. The team finished with an 85–77 **record** and placed third in their **division**. Randy Johnson led the league with 347 strikeouts. He also recorded his 3,000th career strikeout and won his third **Cy Young Award**.

# GRAND SLAMS

THE ARIZONA REPUBLIC
2001
WORLD SERIES
CHAMPIONS

AMERICA WEST
AIRLINES

DIAMOND

Lite

WORLD SERIES
2001

WHEEL OF FORTUNE
The Game's On
3

2001 WORLD CHAMPIONS

The Diamondbacks earned their greatest victory by winning the 2001 World Series. Luis Gonzalez sealed the title with a game-winning **single** against the Yankees. Pitchers Randy Johnson and Curt Schilling were named co-MVPs of the thrilling seven-game series.

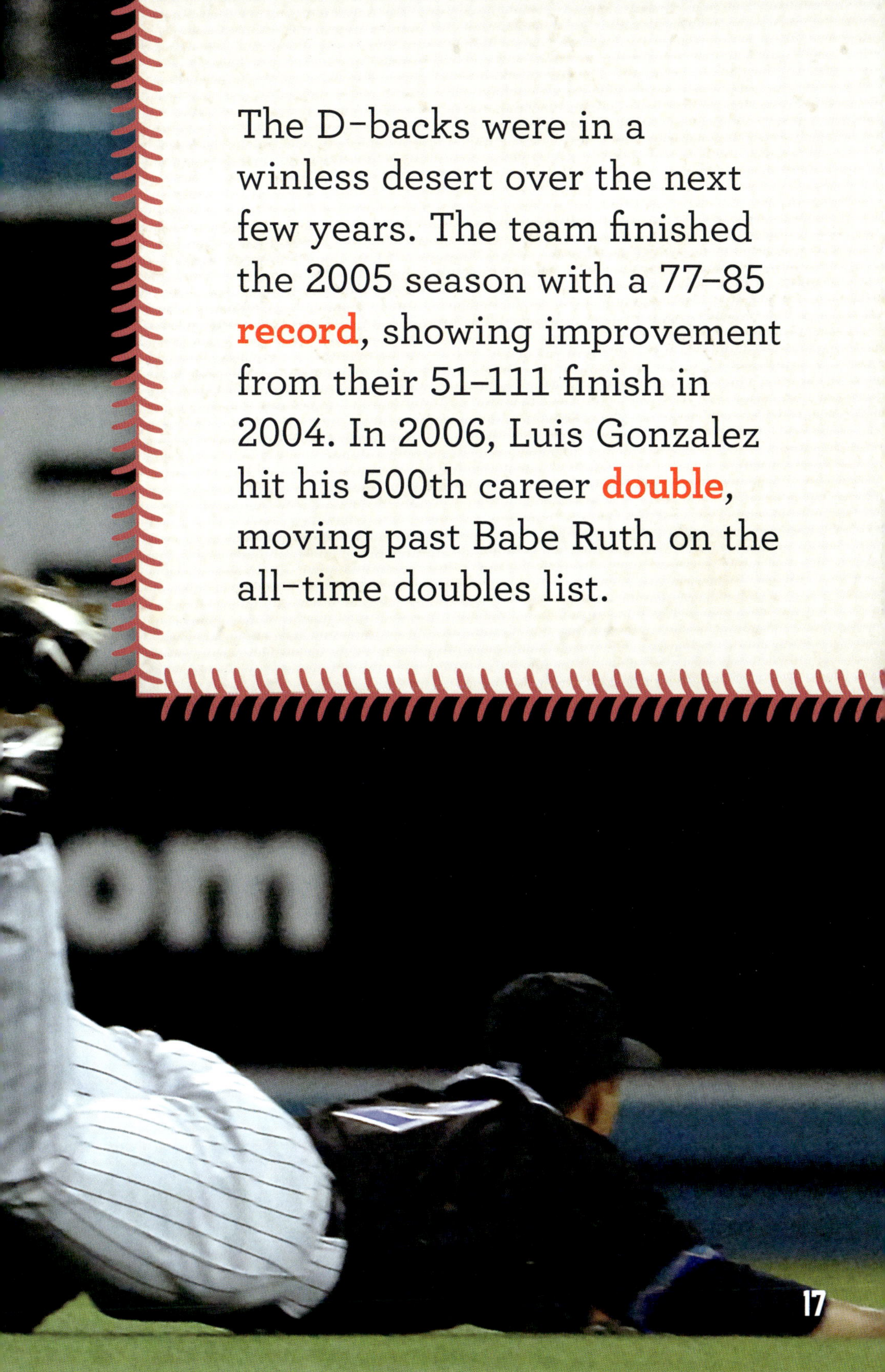

The D-backs were in a winless desert over the next few years. The team finished the 2005 season with a 77–85 **record**, showing improvement from their 51–111 finish in 2004. In 2006, Luis Gonzalez hit his 500th career **double**, moving past Babe Ruth on the all-time doubles list.

Arizona

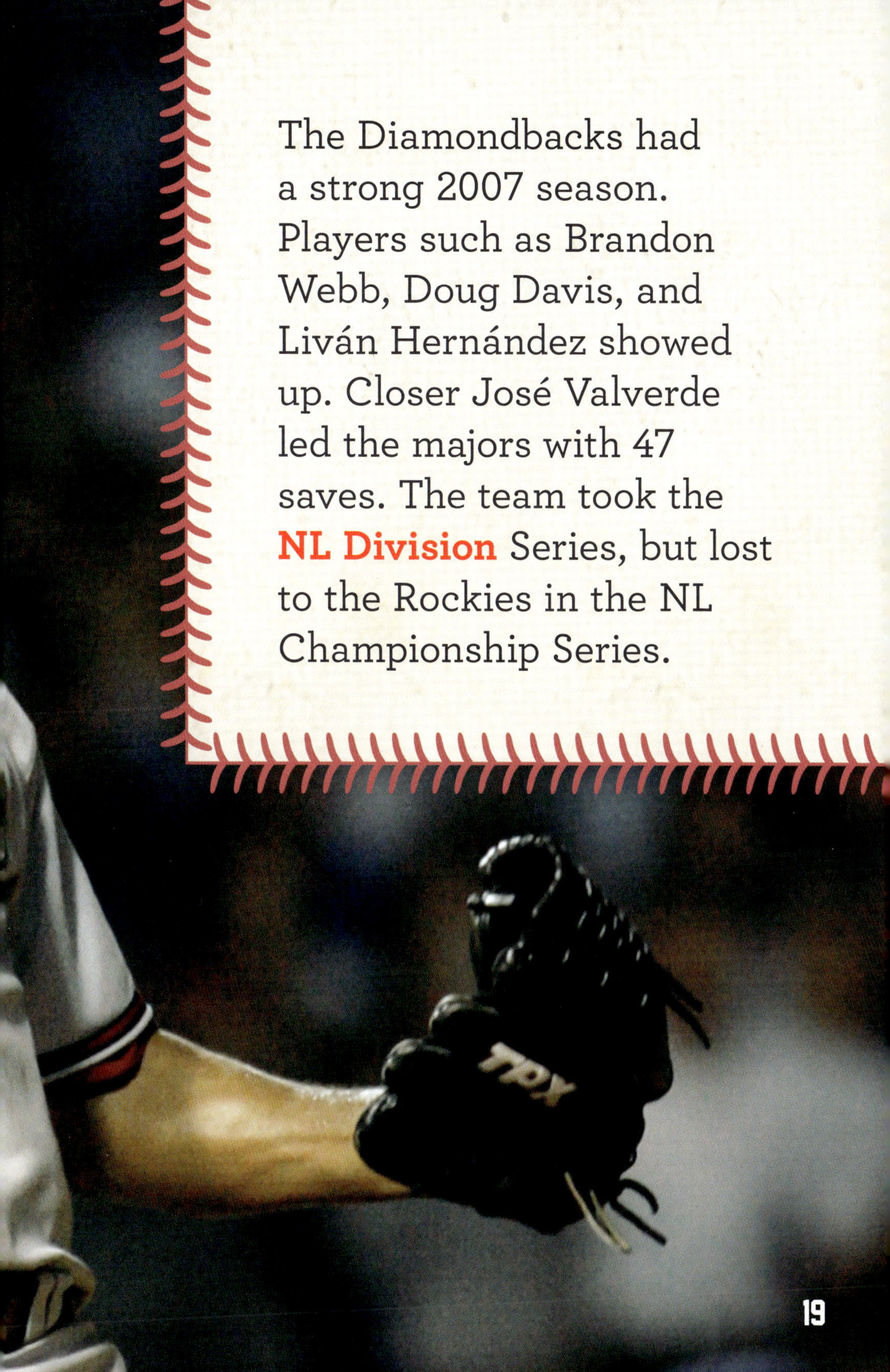


The Diamondbacks had a strong 2007 season. Players such as Brandon Webb, Doug Davis, and Liván Hernández showed up. Closer José Valverde led the majors with 47 saves. The team took the **NL Division** Series, but lost to the Rockies in the NL Championship Series.

In 2011, the Diamondbacks clinched the **NL** West title for the fifth time with a 94–68 **record**. The strong finish earned the team a spot in the playoffs. That season also saw standout pitcher Ian Kennedy become the first in the NL to win 21 games.

scott
NLDS
2011
WEST DIVISION
CHAMPIONS
2011
POSTSEASON

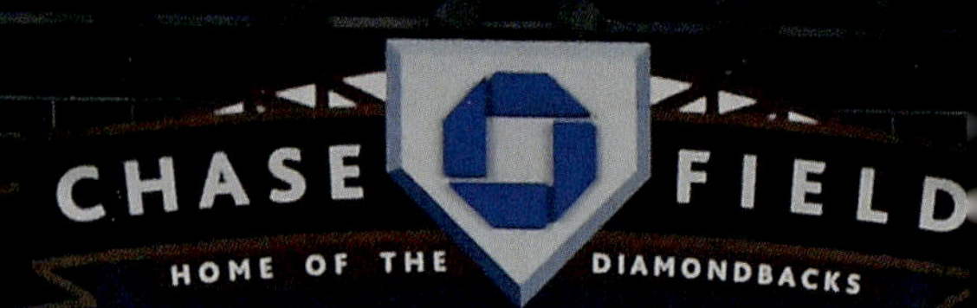

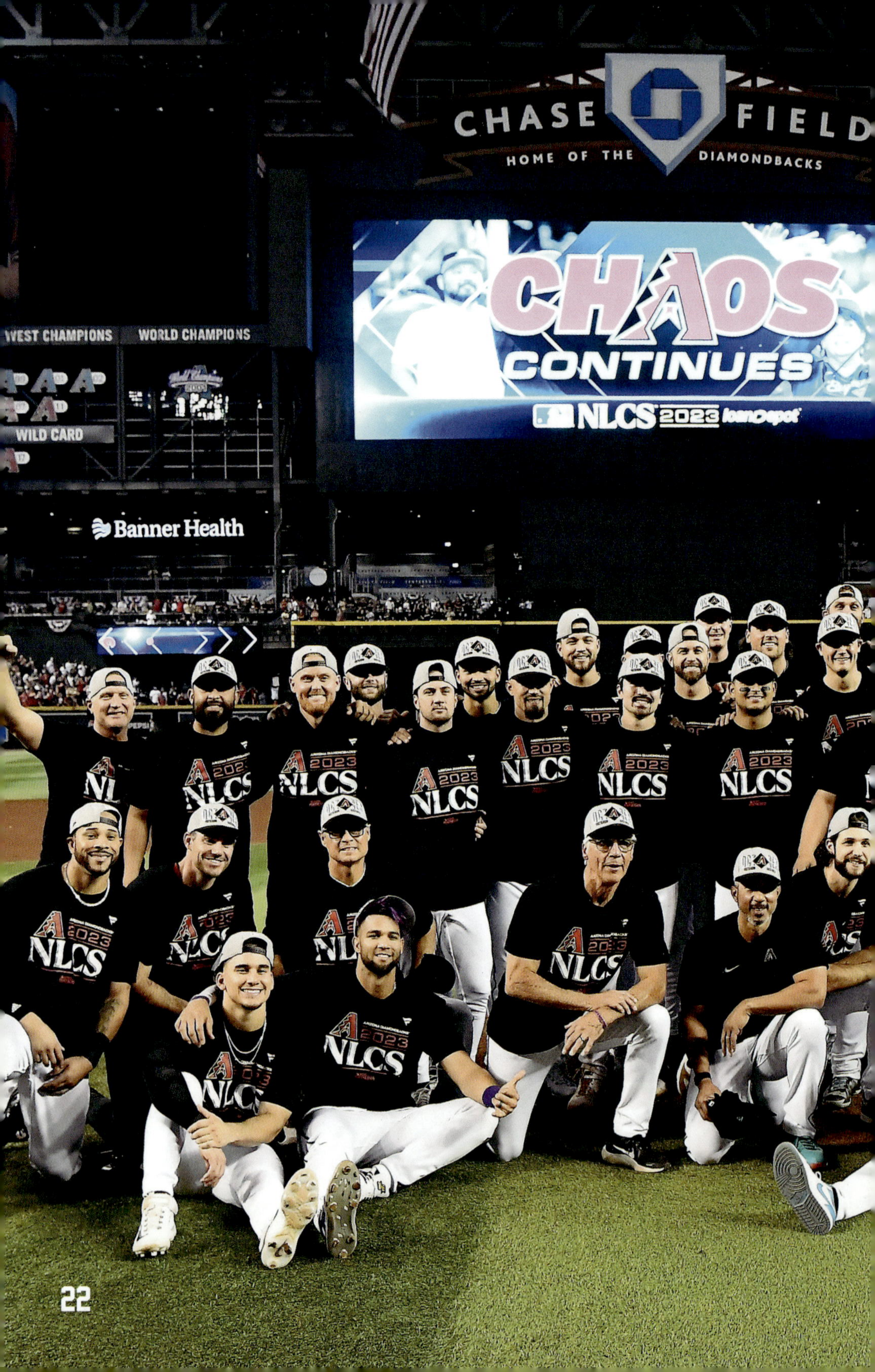
CHASE FIELD
HOME OF THE DIAMONDBACKS
CHAOS
CONTINUES
NLCS 2023 loanDepot
WEST CHAMPIONS
WORLD CHAMPIONS
WILD CARD
Banner Health

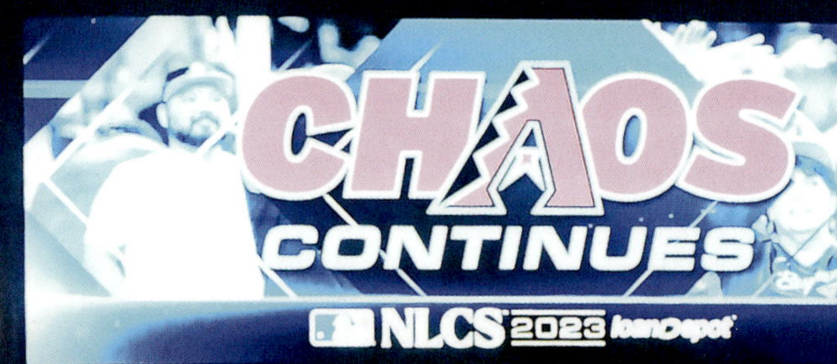

The Diamondbacks beat the Phillies 4–2 in Game 7 of the 2023 **NL** Championship Series, making it to their first World Series since 2001. They lost 4–1 to the Rangers, with the final game played in Arizona.

# HALL OF FAME

The towering 6'10" pitcher Randy Johnson, known as "The Big Unit," was a star for the Diamondbacks. He helped lead the team to a World Series title in 2001.

During his time with Arizona, he earned four **Cy Young Awards** and struck out 2,077 batters with a 2.83 **ERA**. Johnson entered the Baseball Hall of Fame in 2015.

Luis Gonzalez went from outfielder to legend with his **walk-off single** in Game 7 of the 2001 World Series. The same season, he set a team **record** with 57 home runs and earned one of his five **All-Star** selections. Over his career with Arizona, Gonzalez recorded 1,337 hits and 774 **RBIs**.

GOLD GLOVE AWARD
Rawlings
Rawlings

Paul Goldschmidt was a fixture at first base for the Diamondbacks from 2011 to 2018. The right-handed slugger hit for average and power. He led the **NL** with 36 homers and 125 **RBIs** in 2013, the first of his six straight **All-Star** seasons. He earned several awards during his time with the team.

# GLOSSARY

**All-Star** – a yearly baseball contest where top players from the American League (AL) and NL compete against each other.

**Cy Young Award** – an annual American baseball award given to the best pitcher in each of the two MLB leagues.

**division** – a number of teams grouped together in a sport for competitive purposes.

**double** – a type of hit where the batter safely reaches second base on a single play.

**Earned-Run Average (ERA)** – the average number of earned runs per game scored against a pitcher.

**National League (NL)** – one of two 15-team leagues that make up MLB.

**record** – a team's season total of wins and losses; a top achievement by a player or team that no one has done before.

**relatively** – in relation or comparison to something else that is similar.

**Runs Batted In (RBI)** – a statistic that credits a batter for making a play that allows a run to be scored.

**single** – a type of hit where the batter safely reaches first base on a single play.

**walk-off** – any victory in which the home team scores the winning run in the bottom of the final inning.

# ONLINE RESOURCES

To learn more about the Arizona Diamondbacks, please visit **abdobooklinks.com** or scan this QR code. These links are routinely monitored and updated to provide the most current information available.

# INDEX